Menopause Madness

An Empathetic Little Book

Pat Ross

A FIRESIDE BOOK
Published by Simon & Schuster

FIRESIDE
Rockefeller Center
1230 Avenue of the Americas
New York, NY 10020

FIRESIDE and colophon are registered trademarks of Simon & Schuster Inc.

Designed by Kara Hamilton

Manufactured in the United States of America

5   7   9   10   8   6   4

Library of Congress Cataloging-in-Publication Data
Ross, Pat, date.
Menopause madness : an empathetic little book / Pat Ross
p.   cm.
I. Title.
M6231.M453R67   1998   97-39014
818'.5402—dc21   CIP
ISBN 0-684-84227-0

Photo credits:
The Museum of Modern Art Film Stills Archives for pages 21, 31, 43, 83, 91
Courtesy of the Academy of Motion Picture Arts and Sciences for pages
6, 13, 15, 17, 19, 23, 25, 29, 47, 49, 53, 55, 57, 59, 61, 63, 67, 69, 71, 85, 93
The Kobal Collection for pages 9, 11, 35
Margarita Fischer Collection, Department of Special Collections
Ablah Library, Wichita State University for page 45

6

It's time to speak out!
You know you're in menopause when . . .

Your biological clock is beyond repair.

You take hot flashes in stride.

You search for new ways to stay cool at night.

13

Your more unusual friends begin to seem more normal.

Running out of eggs has taken on a whole new meaning.

☞

Those nurturing days are over.

☞

It's a relief to be off the pedestal, but you miss the view.

The rat race has lost its appeal.

You've started to let him know what you want.

☞

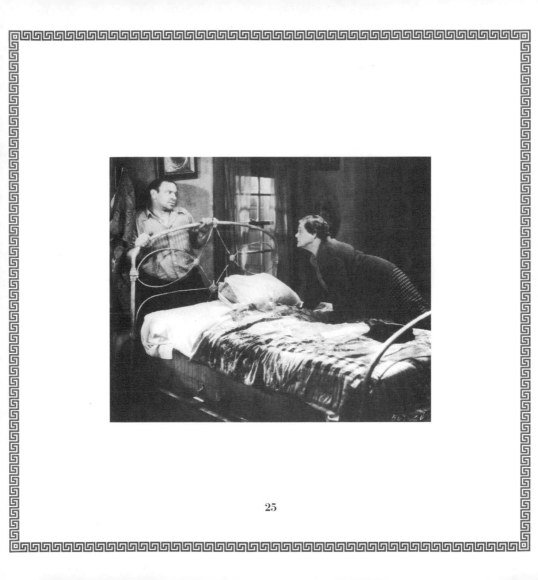

The patch is not part of your sewing kit.

A rapid heartbeat is a daily occurrence.

☞

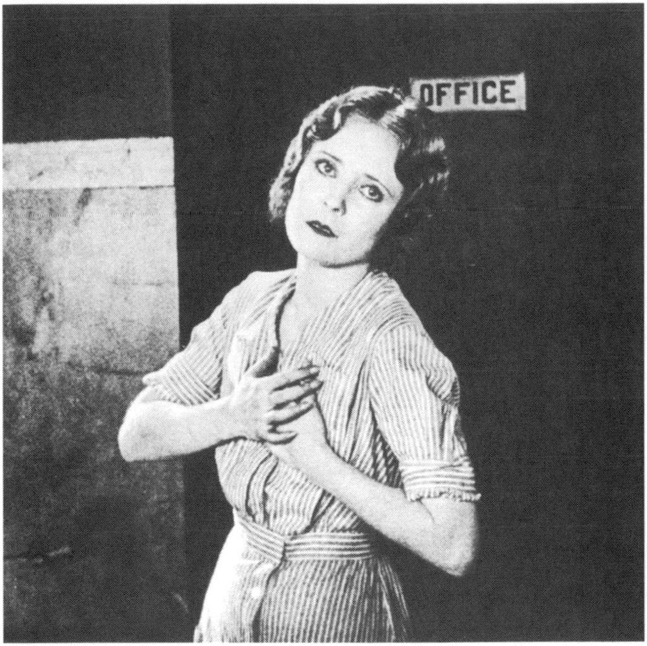
OFFICE

The telephone has become your form of therapy.

You want the men in your life to love your mind.

You finally appreciate your mother.

Lack of estrogen can mean a bad hair day.

☞

You tingle for all the wrong reasons.

☞

39

You're desperate to find something for mood swings.

You need hormones to think straight.

☞

You'd give anything for a good night's sleep.

You need a man who's kind and good-natured—
and it's not him.

You enjoy your own company more with each passing day.

"Hot flash" is just another term for a power surge.

☞

The pull of gravity gets you down.

👉

Your "little laugh lines" are no longer funny.

55

You're considering a face-lift.

No fan is big enough.

☞

Your tendency to faint is misunderstood.

Being late doesn't take you by surprise.

☞

You'd like someone to bring out the animal in you.

Estrogen and a sense of humor get you through.

The man of your dreams has become your worst nightmare.

You make a spectacle of yourself without the usual guilt.

The tightness in your chest is diagnosed as anxiety.

Being at the end of your rope takes on a whole new meaning.

You no longer care about being one of the boys.

You wouldn't think of missing a Girls' Night Out.

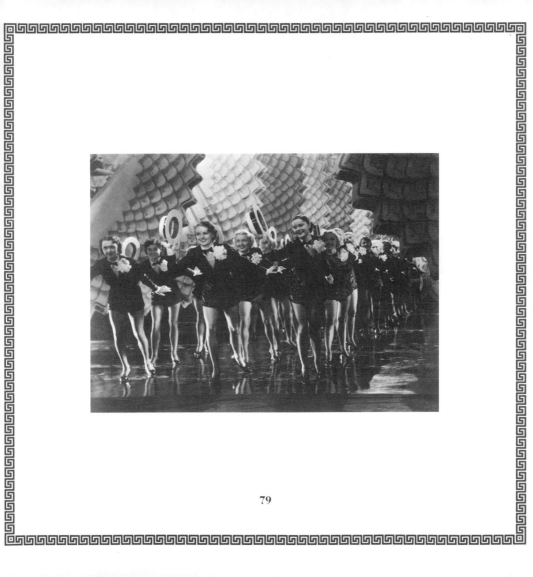

A night on the town really wipes you out.

You no longer fantasize about being swept off your feet.

☞

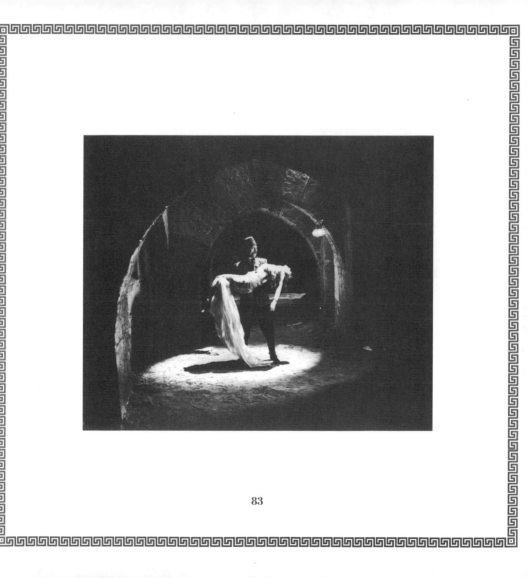

83

A few blemishes take you by surprise.

85

You seem to be retaining fluid for the neighborhood.

You're more interested in where he shops than what he's doing Saturday night.

You're beginning to like yourself for who you are.

You get another cat.

You've finally become a woman who runs with the wolves.